ENCOUNTERS WITH THE PAST

MEET THE
ANCIENT GREEKS

Liz Miles

Gareth Stevens
PUBLISHING

Please visit our website, www.garethstevens.com. For a free color catalog of all our high-quality books, call toll free 1-800-542-2595 or fax 1-877-542-2596.

Miles, Liz.
Meet the ancient Greeks / by Liz Miles.
p. cm. — (Encounters with the past)
Includes index.
ISBN 978-1-4824-0883-6 (pbk.)
ISBN 978-1-4824-0884-3 (6-pack)
ISBN 978-1-4824-0882-9 (library binding)
1. Greece — Civilization — To 146 B.C. — Juvenile literature. I. Miles, Liz. II. Title.
DF77.M55 2015
938—d23

First Edition

Published in 2015 by
Gareth Stevens Publishing
111 East 14th Street, Suite 349
New York, NY 10003

Copyright © Arcturus Holdings Limited

Editors: Joe Harris and Nicola Barber
Design: Elaine Wilkinson
Cover design: Elaine Wilkinson

Cover pictures Shutterstock: temple _LeS_,
mask Repina Valeriya, vase Kamira.
Koryvantes.org: hoplite A.S. Eyzonon.

Picture acknowledgements: Alamy: p12 and title page epa european pressphoto agency b.v.; p19 top North Wind Picture Archives; p23 top Hercules Milas; p26 Ancient Art & Architecture Collection Ltd. Corbis: p25 top Bettmann. Koryvantes.org: pp14, 15 bottom and 24 A. Smaragdis.Melvyn Rawlinson (www.professorpopup.co.uk): p20 and title page (Greek Theatre Project 1997). Shutterstock: p4 background Khunaspix, top inset Lambros Kazan, pot and coins Marques, vase Kamira; pp5 and 28 Mffoto; pp6-7 Portokalis; p6 Igor Bulgarin; p7 top er ryan; p7 bottom Santi Rodriguez; pp8-9 Falk; p8 Igor Bulgarin; p9 top Stefanel; p9 bottom Mountainpix; pp10-11 Kumarin; p10 MIMOHE; p11 top and contents Borisb17; p11 bottom Zerbor; pp12-13 Lambros Kazan; p13 top Dimitrios; pp14-15 and title page Anastasios71; p15 top Olemac; pp16-17 Mike Liu; p16 Puwanai; p17 top Dtopal; p17 bottom Panos Karas; pp18-19 Piotr Papihin; p18 ArtFamily; pp20-21 Bryan Busovicki; p21 top Panos Karas; p21 bottom Dominique Landau; pp22-3 Ventdusud; p22 Igor Bulgarin; p23 bottom Kamira; pp24-5 Anastasios71; p25 bottom dkART; pp26-7 Paul B. Moore; p29 David H. Seymour. Wikimedia Commons: p13 bottom Bibi Saint-Pol; p19 bottom Marie-Lan Nguyen; p27 top Marsyas; p27 bottom Ελληνικά: Χρήστης Templar52; p28 Marie-Lan Nguyen.

Printed in the United States of America

CPSIA compliance information: Batch CS15GS: For further information contact Gareth Stevens, New York, New York at 1-800-542-2595.

Contents

Into the Past

You walk out of a history class, daydreaming. You have been learning about ancient Greece, the "birthplace of Western civilization." The Greeks created a way of life that people have admired and copied ever since. An ancient Greek thinker called Socrates sounds especially interesting.

You're thinking how you would like the chance to talk to Socrates when suddenly a glowing door appears, right in front of you. You hesitate for a moment, then open it. You enter a small, dark room crammed with big clay storage jars. At your feet, there's a basket of clothes and a note.

▲ A fine, decorated vase from ancient Greece. Pottery with red figures and patterns on a black background was developed in the workshops of Athens from around 520BCE.

Your Mission

You are about to enter Athens, the most important city-state in Ancient Greece. The year is 415BCE. The Athenians are at war with Sparta, and Athens is buzzing with ideas and creativity. You have six hours for your mission: to meet people and find out about their lives.

You quickly sort through the clothes and put on a plain linen tunic and a belt. Tied to the belt is a purse containing a few coins. Suddenly another door on the opposite side of the room opens, and the room fills with bright sunshine. Nervously, you step outside … then trip and tumble.

On the Farm

Your journey has started badly – you are in a ditch next to a field of barley, on a farm some distance from the city of Athens! You hear the slash of blades coming towards you. It's a group of slaves, busy harvesting the barley with scythes. You jump up and come face to face with a stern-looking man. As the slaves work, you ask him some questions.

DO YOU OWN THE FARM?

Yes! I normally live in Athens, but I am here to visit my overseer, who looks after the farm for me. This is a big farm and we have slaves to do the heavy work, like harvesting and ploughing, and to work the press that crushes the olives into oil. But there are smaller farms around here, which are owned by families.

WHAT DO YOU GROW ON THE FARM?

In these fields we grow barley, beans, lentils, and fruit, such as pears and pomegranates. We're harvesting the barley now. The grains will be sold to make porridge, or ground into flour to make bread. In autumn, we'll be gathering the olives and grapes that grow further up the slopes where the soil is thinner.

Pomegranates grow well in the hot, dry climate of Greece.

WILL IT BE A GOOD HARVEST?

Yes, I'm sure it will because I went to consult Pythia at the Temple of Apollo, in Delphi. Pythia is a special priestess, known as an oracle, who communicates with the god Apollo. She asks Apollo's advice about all sorts of things – farming matters, or even what will happen in battles. I asked her when was the best time to sow the seeds, and to bring in the harvest.

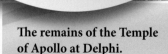

The remains of the Temple of Apollo at Delphi.

A Lift with a Slave

You need to get to the city, so you ask the farm owner for help. He suggests you accompany his overseer on the farm's ox cart, which is just about to set off to Athens with barley to sell. You jump in the back of the wooden cart with one of the slaves – it's an opportunity to find out what a slave's life is really like.

HAVE YOU ALWAYS BEEN A SLAVE?

Like many slaves, I was once a free man. I was a sailor – until pirates ambushed our ship. Then I was taken to Athens and sold as a slave. At first, I worked for an Athenian potter, who treated me well. But then he died and I was sold to the farm owner. My wife is still in Athens. She doesn't know where I am.

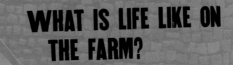

WHAT IS LIFE LIKE ON THE FARM?

The farm overseer works us very hard. We're out in the fields and olive groves every day. It's cold in the winter and very hot in the summer. Even though I had no rights in the city and my marriage wasn't accepted because I am a slave, life in Athens was better than on the farm.

Harvest time in the olive groves.

WILL YOU ALWAYS BE A SLAVE?

I hope not! I am always thinking about how to get back to Athens to find my wife. I learned a lot when I was with the potter, and I hope to use those skills again one day. Then I could make some money. If I saved up enough I could buy myself out of slavery and become a free man. I would not be a citizen, but I would be allowed to live as a *metic* – a foreign resident in Athens.

An ancient Greek pot, decorated with vines.

Refuge in the Workshop

As you enter the city, the slave asks for your help to escape. So, while you distract the overseer, he runs off. But as soon as he realizes what is happening, the furious overseer shouts for soldiers to chase the slave. Fearing they will come after you too, you race down the busy street and into a courtyard. Sculptors and masons are hard at work. You hide behind a half-finished marble figure, and talk to a sculptor who is taking a break.

WHAT ARE YOU WORKING ON?

I'm carving a woman draped in a tunic. I'm trying to make her look realistic, and capture her beauty. We Greeks think it's a mark of a great artist to capture a lifelike image of a real person. The statue is going to act as a pillar, holding up a roof, so strength is built into the design. This kind of statue is called a caryatid.

WHERE WILL IT GO?

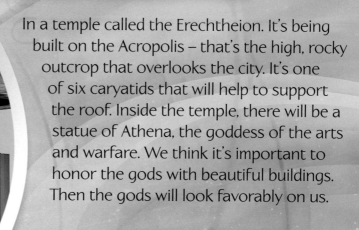

In a temple called the Erechtheion. It's being built on the Acropolis – that's the high, rocky outcrop that overlooks the city. It's one of six caryatids that will help to support the roof. Inside the temple, there will be a statue of Athena, the goddess of the arts and warfare. We think it's important to honor the gods with beautiful buildings. Then the gods will look favorably on us.

The caryatids hold up the roof of the north porch of the Erechtheion.

WHO TAUGHT YOU?

Like all trainee sculptors, I started out as an apprentice. I was taught how to use these chisels and mallets by one of Phidias's students. Phidias died several years ago, but he is my inspiration – he was the greatest sculptor in Greece. He directed the building and carvings on the Acropolis, and he sculpted the massive figure of Athena that stands in the main temple, the Parthenon.

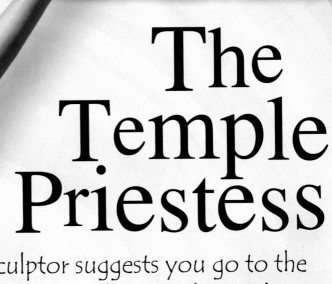

The Temple Priestess

The sculptor suggests you go to the Acropolis and look at the Parthenon. As you climb the rocky path, you hear people talking about a festival that happened the day before. You make your way into the Parthenon, where you meet a priestess. She is happy to answer your questions.

WHAT DO YOU DO IN THE TEMPLE?

I help with the temple rituals. I give offerings of water, milk, oil, or honey to the gods in order to please them. When I pray to Apollo and the other gods, I raise my hands to the sky. Some priests and priestesses are trained to read omens – signs from the gods. They come in flashes of lightning, for example, or in the patterns made by birds as they fly.

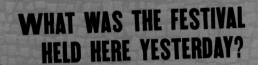

WHAT WAS THE FESTIVAL HELD HERE YESTERDAY?

It was the Panathenaea festival, which is held once a year. It's in honor of the goddess Athena. There was a great procession up to the Acropolis to drape a new cloak on the statue of Athena in the Parthenon. Every fourth year, there's a much bigger Panathenaea festival with lots of music, dancing, and sporting contests.

Athena, goddess of wisdom and warfare, and protector of the city of Athens.

ARE THERE MALE PRIESTS IN THE TEMPLE TOO?

Yes, there are male and female priests in Athens, and we have equal power in the temples. Some priests and priestesses, such as Pythia, the oracle at Delphi, are very influential. However, most of us are no more important than ordinary people.

A visitor to Pythia, the oracle, in Delphi.
Pythia was an important figure in ancient Greece.

Talking to the Archer

Walking out of the dark temple, you're momentarily blinded by the bright sun. You hear someone shout, "Look out!" and an arrow sweeps past your ear! You've stepped in front of a small tree being used by an archer for target practice. As you recover from your near miss, the archer shows off his skills. You decide to ask him some questions.

WHY ARE YOU SUCH A GOOD ARCHER?

Like all my friends, when I finished school I had two years of military training as an *ephebe* – that's a youth aged between 18 and 20. I had to take the *ephebic* oath to respect our rulers and defend the rights of gods and men. We were all taught how to use weapons and to march. At the end of the second year of training, I became a citizen.

MIGHT YOU HAVE TO GO TO WAR?

I have already been in battle, against the Spartans. We archers fought alongside the hoplites – these are soldiers armed with spears and shields. Many of them wear heavy metal armor, as well as helmets. Unlike the hoplites, the archers don't have armor, but we do carry shields to give us some protection.

The figures on this vase show a hoplite fighting an opponent.

DOES THE ARMY HAVE OTHER WEAPONS?

The archers fight alongside javelin throwers and slingers. Javelins have a sharp metal point on the end, and with skill, a slinger can fling a rock and knock out an enemy soldier. The hoplites carry round shields that they can lock together to form a protective barrier. This is called a phalanx formation.

Olympic Escape

You hear the noise of a group of men approaching. It's a search party, led by the overseer, looking for the slave. The overseer sees you and shouts. You run as fast as you can down the Acropolis. Then you realize you aren't alone – a youth is running alongside you. He guides you into a maze of streets where you quickly lose the search party. As soon as it's safe, you stop to catch your breath. Then you ask the youth some questions.

YOU'RE A FAST RUNNER! WHAT DO YOU DO?

I'm an athlete. I was the torchbearer who carried the sacred flame at yesterday's Panathenaea festival. Sport is very important here in Greece. Every four years, the Olympic Games are held on the plains of Olympia. It's an amazing event – even wars stop for the Olympics! We compete in honor of Zeus, king of all gods and goddesses.

HAVE YOU WON ANY RACES?

I won the stade, a one-length sprint of the stadium. As a prize, I was given a wreath made from laurel. I received gifts from citizens who wanted to show their admiration, too. One day I hope to compete in the pentathlon, which includes running, wrestling, long jump, and throwing the javelin and the discus.

This vase shows ancient Greek athletes in a race.

WHICH SPORTS ARE THE MOST EXCITING AT THE OLYMPICS?

I like to watch the boxing, but chariot races are the most exciting. There are races for two- and four-horse chariots. They do 12 laps of the hippodrome. It's amazing to watch up to 40 chariots charging around, often crashing into each other. The fallen charioteers sometimes get dragged under the chariot wheels.

A four-horse chariot competes in a race at the hippodrome.

17

A Greek Home

The athlete invites you to his parents' home for a cold drink. You enter the courtyard of a large, two-floored house. The athlete's mother, dressed in a long tunic called a *chiton*, ushers you past a colorful, mosaic-floored room. You ask her some questions as she leads you to the kitchen.

HOW MANY ROOMS DOES YOUR HOUSE HAVE?

We have more than most! Downstairs is the *andron*, which we passed. It's used mainly by my husband and his friends for meetings and meals. There's a kitchen and bathroom too. The bedrooms are upstairs, as well as the servants' rooms and my *gynaecium* where I spend a lot of time spinning and organizing the household.

WHAT DO YOU DO ALL DAY?

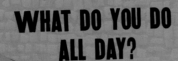

My women friends visit most days and we sit together in my private room, the *gynaecium*, exchanging news. But like all women in Athens, I'm not allowed to take part in the government of our city. The servants run my errands and help me prepare for social events, such as the symposium my husband is hosting this evening.

WHAT IS A SYMPOSIUM?

It's a social gathering for my husband and his guests, where they discuss everything from politics to poetry. As a woman I am not permitted to go, but I make sure the servants provide plenty of food and wine. Tonight we will serve fish, meat, and fruit, and I have hired dancers and musicians to entertain the guests while they eat.

Behind the Mask

After a drink of water, you say your goodbyes and step outside. Suddenly a grimacing face leaps at you from the shadows. It's a young man wearing a mask, and he laughs as he removes it. He's the athlete's cousin, an actor, and he's on his way to the theater to rehearse. You decide to go along with him to find out more.

WHAT PLAY ARE YOU IN?

I'm in the *Oresteia*, a series of three tragedies by our great dramatic poet, Aeschylus. Some years ago, the plays won a prize at the city's drama festival. The festival is held every year in honor of the god Dionysus. All the actors are men. I'm playing the part of King Agamemnon on his return home from the Trojan Wars.

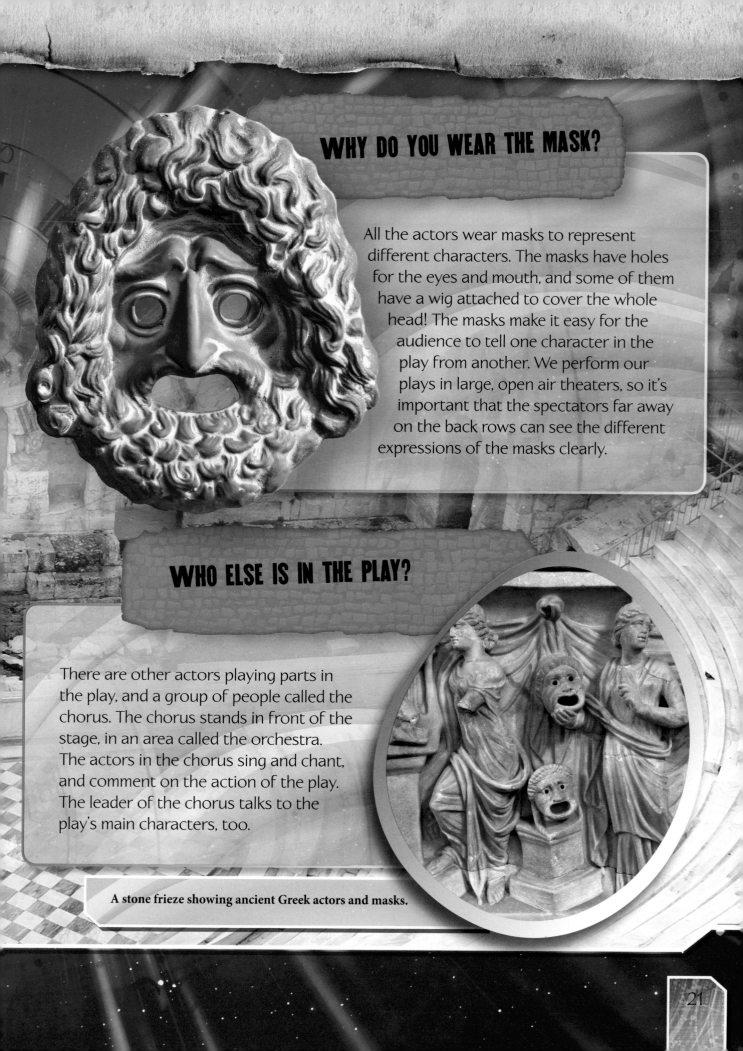

WHY DO YOU WEAR THE MASK?

All the actors wear masks to represent different characters. The masks have holes for the eyes and mouth, and some of them have a wig attached to cover the whole head! The masks make it easy for the audience to tell one character in the play from another. We perform our plays in large, open air theaters, so it's important that the spectators far away on the back rows can see the different expressions of the masks clearly.

WHO ELSE IS IN THE PLAY?

There are other actors playing parts in the play, and a group of people called the chorus. The chorus stands in front of the stage, in an area called the orchestra. The actors in the chorus sing and chant, and comment on the action of the play. The leader of the chorus talks to the play's main characters, too.

A stone frieze showing ancient Greek actors and masks.

Meeting the Philosopher

Just as you arrive at the theater, you hear a crash. You find a small crowd talking to a man who looks vaguely familiar. Suddenly you recognize him! It's Socrates! The crash came from a broken pot, thrown in anger at the philosopher by a furious man. You rush forward and beg to ask Socrates a few questions.

WHY WAS THAT MAN ANGRY WITH YOU?

The man was cross because I was encouraging his son to question the beliefs of his parents. He is not the only person to be angry with me. Many people think I am dangerous because I discuss everything, and I encourage others to do the same. I even ask questions about our Athenian democracy and whether our leaders have enough knowledge to rule.

HOW DOES DEMOCRACY WORK IN ATHENS?

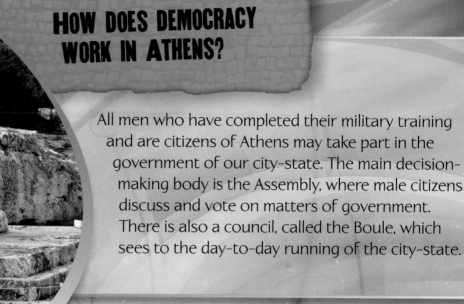

All men who have completed their military training and are citizens of Athens may take part in the government of our city-state. The main decision-making body is the Assembly, where male citizens discuss and vote on matters of government. There is also a council, called the Boule, which sees to the day-to-day running of the city-state.

The speaker's platform at the Pnyx in Athens, where the Athenian Assembly met.

WHAT OTHER THINGS DO YOU DISCUSS?

I ask such questions as: "What is justice?" "What is goodness?" Discussion of these questions often shows the lack of logic in many popular beliefs. I have a great many followers who are interested in what I have to say. I don't accept payment for my discussions, so I'm quite poor, but I don't mind because I think knowledge and the mind are more important than material things.

A stone head of Socrates.

Soldiers on the March

You leave Socrates to his discussions, but as you make your way down the street you feel a heavy hand on your shoulder. It's a hoplite. He growls at you, "You helped the slave escape!" Suddenly there's a shout – the soldiers are being ordered to board their ships. "You're coming with me!" says the hoplite. But he agrees to answer your questions as you march.

HOW DID YOU BECOME A HOPLITE?

I did my two years of military training as an *ephebe*. Afterwards, because my family had enough money for my weapons and armor, I became an elite foot soldier – a hoplite, rather than an ordinary soldier such as an archer or javelin thrower.

WHO IS YOUR ENEMY?

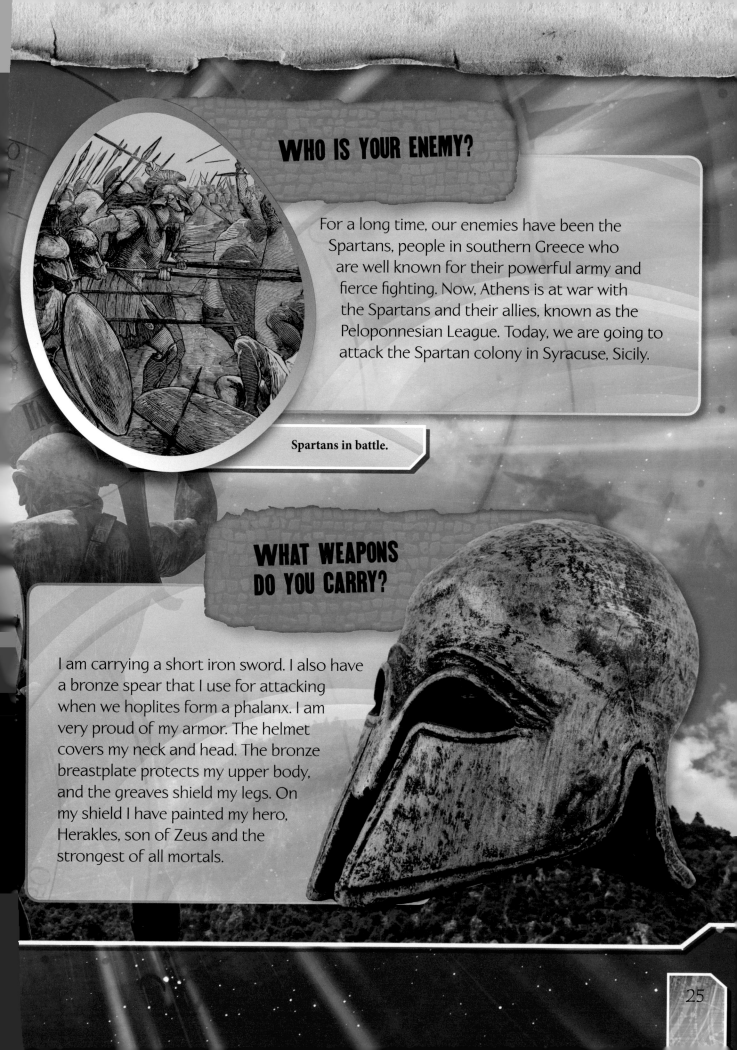

For a long time, our enemies have been the Spartans, people in southern Greece who are well known for their powerful army and fierce fighting. Now, Athens is at war with the Spartans and their allies, known as the Peloponnesian League. Today, we are going to attack the Spartan colony in Syracuse, Sicily.

Spartans in battle.

WHAT WEAPONS DO YOU CARRY?

I am carrying a short iron sword. I also have a bronze spear that I use for attacking when we hoplites form a phalanx. I am very proud of my armor. The helmet covers my neck and head. The bronze breastplate protects my upper body, and the greaves shield my legs. On my shield I have painted my hero, Herakles, son of Zeus and the strongest of all mortals.

The Trireme Oarsman

You arrive at the port. It's very busy with soldiers waiting to board the ships, called triremes, that are lined up along the quay. In the confusion, you manage to slip away from the hoplite. You only have a little time left, but you linger to talk to one of the trireme oarsmen.

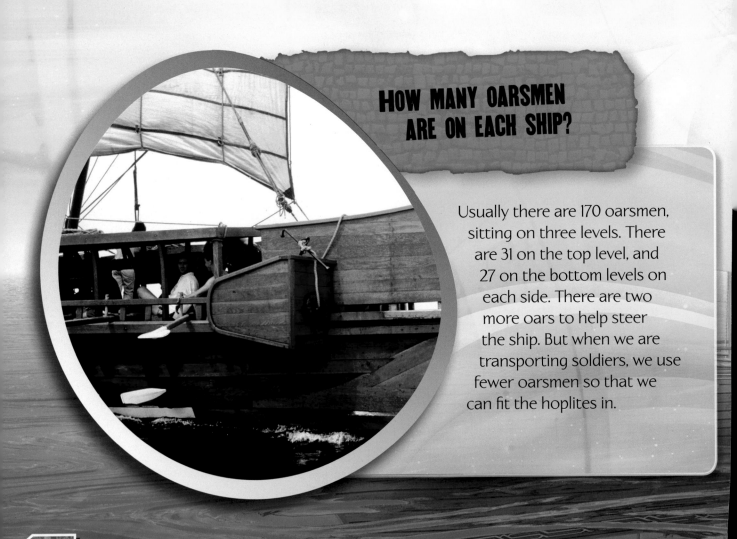

HOW MANY OARSMEN ARE ON EACH SHIP?

Usually there are 170 oarsmen, sitting on three levels. There are 31 on the top level, and 27 on the bottom levels on each side. There are two more oars to help steer the ship. But when we are transporting soldiers, we use fewer oarsmen so that we can fit the hoplites in.

ARE TRIREMES GOOD WARSHIPS?

They are the best! With a full crew of oarsmen, the trireme is very fast. We have a sail to help us, but we don't have to wait for a good wind. The oars also make it easy to steer the trireme, so we can do quick maneuvers.

This stone frieze shows part of a three-layered trireme.

DO YOU HAVE SPECIAL TACTICS?

The trick is to head fast into the side or back of an enemy ship! The front of the trireme is specially shaped and strengthened with bronze to act as a battering ram. If we ram an enemy ship with enough speed and force, the ram will pierce a hole, so that the ship sinks in minutes.

Back to the Present

The triremes are leaving the quayside, and you are running out of time to get back to the present. Someone tugs your arm – it's the slave! He quickly explains that he has found his wife and that he's safe. He thrusts a parcel into your hands and runs off. As soon as you unwrap the parcel and touch the pot inside, there's a flash of light and you're back in the 21st century.

WHAT HAPPENED TO SOCRATES?

You find out that Plato, one of Socrates' students, recorded the life of the philosopher. You read that in 399BCE, Socrates was put on trial for "corrupting the youth" by encouraging young people to question everything. He was found guilty and sentenced to death by drinking a deadly poison, called hemlock. Today, Socrates, Plato, and Plato's student Aristotle are considered to be the founders of Western philosophy and science.

Plato was a student of Socrates.

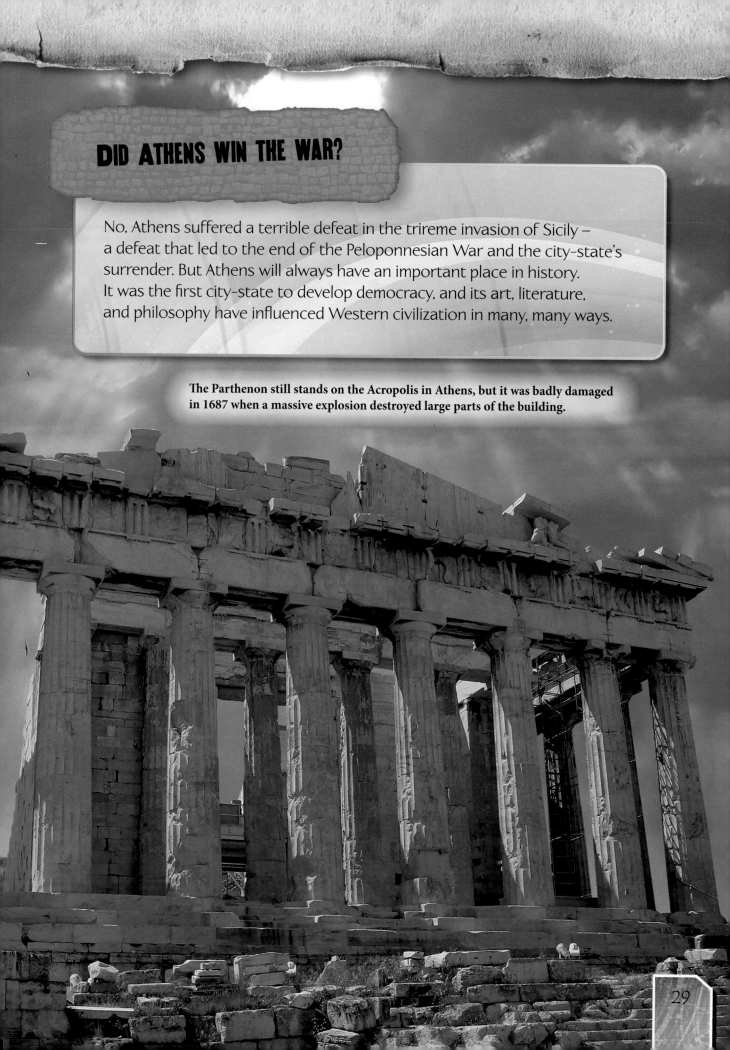

DID ATHENS WIN THE WAR?

No, Athens suffered a terrible defeat in the trireme invasion of Sicily – a defeat that led to the end of the Peloponnesian War and the city-state's surrender. But Athens will always have an important place in history. It was the first city-state to develop democracy, and its art, literature, and philosophy have influenced Western civilization in many, many ways.

The Parthenon still stands on the Acropolis in Athens, but it was badly damaged in 1687 when a massive explosion destroyed large parts of the building.

Glossary

Acropolis (of Athens) A group of ancient ruined buildings on a high, rocky outcrop above the city of Athens in Greece.

andron In ancient Greece, a part of a house reserved for men only (apart from female entertainers such as dancers).

Apollo The ancient Greek god of the sun, light and truth, patron of the shrine at Delphi.

Assembly The main decision-making body in ancient Athens. Members of the Assembly, all male citizens, discussed and voted on matters of the city-state.

Athena The goddess of the arts and warfare, and the protector of the city of Athens.

caryatid A sculpture of a female figure that is used to support the roof of a building.

chiton A long or short tunic worn by men or women in ancient Greece, made from a single cloth wrapped around and belted, and fastened at one or both shoulders.

citizen In the Athenian city-state, a man over the age of 18 who had completed his *ephebic* training. Citizens were allowed to vote, and held certain responsibilities, such as volunteering for jury service in the Athenian courts.

city-state A small nation made up of a city and the surrounding land, such as Athens and Sparta.

democracy A form of government by the people.

Dionysus The ancient Greek god of wine harvests, wine, plays, and drunken revelry.

discus A heavy disc that is thrown in competition.

ephebe In ancient Greece, a male youth aged between 18 and 20.

gynaecium In ancient Greece, a part of a house reserved for women only.

hippodrome A racetrack used for horse and chariot racing.

hoplite A Greek soldier-citizen.

laurel wreath A crown made from the leaves of the bay laurel bush, which represented victory.

metic A person living in Athens who was not from Greece, and who did not have citizenship.

Olympia The site in western Greece of the ancient Olympic Games.

Olympics A sporting contest held every four years by the ancient Greeks in honor of Zeus.

omen A sign from the gods.

oracle In ancient times, an oracle was a priest or priestess who was thought to communicate directly with the gods to predict the future. The most famous oracle was at Delphi.

Parthenon The main temple on the Acropolis, dedicated to Athena.

phalanx A military formation made up of hoplites using their shields to form a protective barrier.

Pythia The name of the priestess who was the oracle at Delphi.

scythe A sharp, curved blade with a wooden handle, used to cut grass or crops.

Sparta An ancient Greek city-state, famous for its army.

symposium A social gathering for ancient Greek men, which included food, drink, and discussion of a wide range of topics.

Zeus The father of the Greek gods, and god of the sky and thunder.

For More Information

WEBSITES

http://acropolis-virtualtour.gr/
An interactive virtual tour of the four main buildings on the Acropolis.

http://www.ancientgreece.co.uk/
The British Museum interactive website, including photos, stories, and games.

http://www.ancient-greece.org/architecture.html
A timeline and photos of Greek architecture and challenges.

http://www.hoplites.org/
The Hoplite Association is an organization that re-enacts Classical Greek life.

http://www.mythweb.com/
Heroes, gods, and monsters of Ancient Greece.

BOOKS

Ancient Greece (Eyewitness Project Books) (Dorling Kindersley, 2009)

The British Museum Pocket Timeline of Ancient Greece by Emma McAllister (British Museum Press, 2005)

The Groovy Greeks (Horrible Histories) by Terry Deary (Scholastic 2007)

Men, Women and Children: In Ancient Greece by Colin Hynson (Wayland, 2009)

The Parthenon: The Height of Greek Civilization (Wonders of the World) by Elizabeth Mann (Miyaka Press, 2007)

Tales of the Greek Heroes (Puffin Classics) by Roger Lancelyn Green (Puffin, 2012)

Index